JS

HARTLEPOOL BOROUGH
WITHDRAWN
LIBRARIES

D0236128

Physical Science

Light

by Abbie Dunne

a Capstone company — publishers for children

Raintree is an imprint of Capstone Global Library Limited, a company incorporated in England and Wales having its registered office at 264 Banbury Road, Oxford, OX2 7DY – Registered company number: 6695582

www.raintree.co.uk
myorders@raintree.co.uk

Text © Capstone Global Library Limited 2017
The moral rights of the proprietor have been asserted.

All rights reserved. No part of this publication may be reproduced in any form or by any means (including photocopying or storing it in any medium by electronic means and whether or not transiently or incidentally to some other use of this publication) without the written permission of the copyright owner, except in accordance with the provisions of the Copyright, Designs and Patents Act 1988 or under the terms of a licence issued by the Copyright Licensing Agency, Saffron House, 6–10 Kirby Street, London EC1N 8TS (www.cla.co.uk). Applications for the copyright owner's written permission should be addressed to the publisher.

Edited by Linda Staniford
Designed by Veronica Scott
Picture research by Eric Gohl
Production by Katy LaVigne

ISBN 978 1 474 72246 9
20 19 18 17 16
10 9 8 7 6 5 4 3 2 1

British Library Cataloguing in Publication Data
A full catalogue record for this book is available from the British Library.

Acknowledgements
We would like to thank the following for permission to reproduce photographs: Shutterstock: cocoangel, 13, Gelpi JM, 5, iconizer, 20 (mug), J. Palys, 11, leolintang, 9, LiAndStudio, 19, Michael C. Gray, 15, Monticello, 20 (jar), Ron Dale, 20 (glass), Sabphoto, cover, S_E, 7, wizdata1, 17
Design Elements: Shutterstock

Every effort has been made to contact copyright holders of material reproduced in this book. Any omissions will be rectified in subsequent printings if notice is given to the publisher.

All the Internet addresses (URLs) given in this book were valid at the time of going to press. However, due to the dynamic nature of the Internet, some addresses may have changed, or sites may have changed or ceased to exist since publication. While the author and publisher regret any inconvenience this may cause readers, no responsibility for any such changes can be accepted by either the author or the publisher.

Printed and bound in China.

Contents

What is light?

Light is energy that travels
in a ray. Light bounces off
things and goes into our eyes.
This is how we see things.

Sources of light

Light comes from many sources. The largest light source is the sun. The moon and stars make light too. So do lightbulbs, candles and TVs.

Transparent or translucent?

Transparent things are clear.

They let all light through.

We see clearly through a

transparent glass window.

Translucent things scatter some light. Things look blurry through coloured glass because it is translucent.

Blocking or reflecting?

Some things, such as wood and rocks, don't let any light through. They are opaque. We can't see through these things.

Other things are shiny.

Light is bounced off them,

or reflected. A mirror

reflects a lot of light.

You can see yourself in it.

What is colour?

Imagine a white sheet of paper coloured with crayons. The finished page has many colours. We see colours because objects reflect light.

Some light is reflected off an object. The colour light that reflects is the colour we see. Green light reflects off grass, so grass looks green.

Activity

Have you wondered what kinds of items make shadows?

Do this activity to find out which items make shadows and why.

What you need

- 3 sheets of paper
- pencil
- book
- white index card
- objects that are transparent, translucent and opaque
- torch
- pencil and paper for making notes
- digital camera or crayons and paper

translucent

transparent

opaque

What you do

1. On one sheet of paper, write "transparent=light passes through."

2. Write "translucent=some light passes through" at the top of another sheet of paper.

3. Write "opaque=no light passes through" on the third sheet. Set aside.

4. Put the book on the table in front of you. Stand the index card against it.

5. Put the first object about an arm's length in front of the index card.

6. Turn on the torch. Shine the light on the front of the object.

7. See how much light shines through the object onto the card. Is there a shadow? Take notes.

8. Put the object on the piece of paper that describes it.

9. Repeat until all of your objects are sorted into the correct piles.

10. Draw a picture of the piles, or use a camera to take a picture of them.

What do you think?

Make a claim.

A claim is something you believe to be true.

What kinds of objects make shadows? Why? Use the results of the experiment to support your claim.

Glossary

opaque letting no light pass through

ray line of light that beams out from something bright

reflect return light from an object

scatter separate something into smaller pieces and send it in many different directions

shadow dark shape made when something blocks light

source place where something begins

translucent letting some light through

transparent letting all light through

Find out more
Books

All About Light (All About Science), Angela Royston (Raintree, 2016)

Experiments in Light and Sound with Toys and Everyday Stuff (Fun Science), Natalie Rompella (Raintree, 2015)

Light (Moving Up with Science), Peter Riley (Franklin Watts, 2016)

Websites

www.bbc.co.uk/bitesize/ks2/science/physical_processes/light/read/1/

Find out more about sources of light and how we see things.

www.bbc.co.uk/bitesize/quiz/q44852863

This site has a quiz about light.

resources.woodlands-junior.kent.sch.uk/revision/science/lightshadows.html

This site has interactive games and activities about light.

Comprehension questions

1. Why can we see clearly through a transparent glass window?

2. Wood and rocks are opaque. What does this mean?

3. Grass looks green because green light reflects off of it.
   Why do you think a pumpkin looks orange?

Index